# Independence Day

**by Marc Tyler Nobleman**

Content Adviser: Alton Hornsby Jr., Ph.D.,
Fuller E. Callaway, Professor of History, Morehouse College, Atlanta, Georgia

Reading Adviser: Susan Kesselring, M.A., Literacy Educator,
Rosemount-Apple Valley-Eagan (Minnesota) School District

**Let's See Library**
**Compass Point Books**
**Minneapolis, Minnesota**

Compass Point Books
3109 West 50th Street, #115
Minneapolis, MN 55410

Visit Compass Point Books on the Internet at *www.compasspointbooks.com*
or e-mail your request to *custserv@compasspointbooks.com*

On the cover: Fireworks over the Capitol in Washington, D.C.

Photographs ©: Pete Saloutos/Corbis, cover; Comstock, 4; Skjold Photographs, 6; Time Life Pictures/Mansell/Getty Images,
8; Stock Montage, Inc., 10; Photodisc, 12; North Wind Picture Archives, 14; William Thomas Cain/Getty Images, 16;
Earl & Nazima Kowall/Corbis, 18; John Elk III, 20.

Creative Director: Terri Foley
Managing Editor: Catherine Neitge
Editor: Brenda Haugen
Photo Researcher: Marcie C. Spence
Designers: Melissa Kes and Les Tranby
Educational Consultant: Diane Smolinski

**Library of Congress Cataloging-in-Publication Data**
Nobleman, Marc Tyler.
    Independence Day / by Marc Tyler Nobleman.
        p. cm. — (Let's see)
    Includes index.
    ISBN 0-7565-0769-3
    1. Fourth of July—Juvenile literature. 2. Fourth of July celebrations—Juvenile literature. 3. United States—
History—Revolution, 1775-1783—Juvenile literature. I. Title. II. Series.
    E286.A147 2005
    973.3'13—dc22                                    2004005086

# Table of Contents

NOTE: In this book, words that are defined in the glossary
are in **bold** the first time they appear in the text.

4

# What Is Independence Day?

**Independence** Day is celebrated as the birthday of the United States. It is a national holiday.

Americans celebrate freedom on Independence Day. Some Americans gather for community celebrations. Others enjoy the holiday with their friends or family. Wherever they are on Independence Day, Americans remember how the United States of America began. They talk about how it feels to be an American.

◄ *A cake is decorated for Independence Day.*

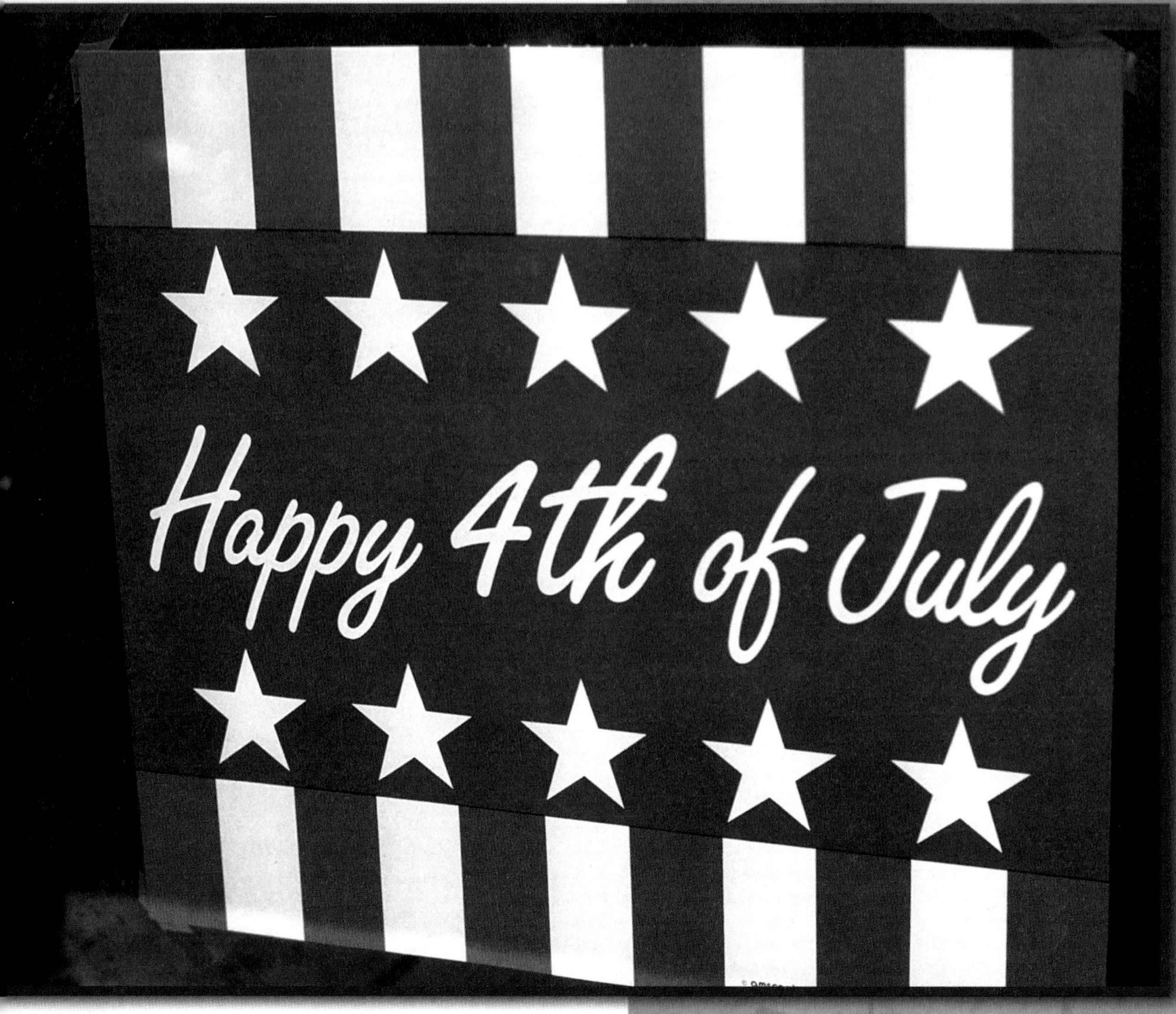
Happy 4th of July

# When Is Independence Day?

Independence Day is on July 4 every year. That date is the **anniversary** of a famous event. It is the date the United States became a country.

　　Most people do not have to work on Independence Day. Post offices and government offices are closed. Since Independence Day is in the summer, most schools are already closed.

◀ *A sign on a business's window*

# How Did Independence Day Begin?

What became the United States used to be made up of 13 **colonies** ruled by Great Britain. The **colonists** became angry when the British taxed them to help pay for a war with France.

The colonists wanted to be free to make their own decisions. They began fighting with the British in 1775. That was the start of the American Revolution, or the Revolutionary War.

A group of colonists met in Philadelphia in 1776. They agreed to break free from Great Britain's rule. This is the event Americans celebrate on Independence Day.

◀ *British soldiers and American colonists fight in a Revolutionary War battle.*

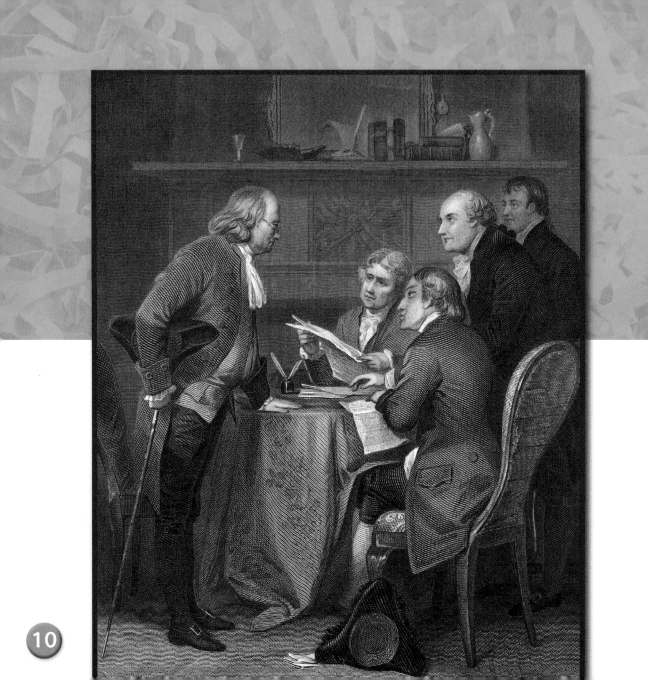

# What Is the Declaration of Independence?

The American colonists wrote the Declaration of Independence and sent it to the British king. This important paper said why the colonists wanted to be free.

Thomas Jefferson wrote the first **draft** of the declaration. Benjamin Franklin, John Adams, and other men also wrote parts. The colonial leaders approved the declaration on July 4, 1776.

The declaration did not make the colonists free right away. Their war with the British lasted until 1783. Then the colonies became 13 states, and the colonists were free. The United States was born.

◄ Thomas Jefferson, second from left, talks to others helping him write the Declaration of Independence.

# How Is Independence Day Celebrated in the U.S.?

Independence Day is a happy time for most Americans. The weather is usually warm. Many people spend time outdoors. People may go to parades, concerts, or festivals. Some families have picnics or backyard barbecues. They eat hot dogs, hamburgers, and corn on the cob. Others may go to a beach or play sports. At night, crowds of people watch colorful fireworks displays.

◀ *Children enjoy an Independence Day barbecue in the park.*

# How Has Independence Day Changed?

The first Independence Day celebration was in Philadelphia in 1777. Ships in the harbor fired their cannons 13 times, once for each state. People lit candles and built **bonfires.** They rang bells and flew flags. They even set off firecrackers.

The holiday became popular in many places in the early 1800s. Some people went to big, fancy dinners. Some listened to speeches.

Today, Independence Day is about **patriotism.** Americans show they love their country. Many other Independence Day **traditions** from the past are still part of the celebration.

◄ A July 4th gathering in the 1860s featured patriotic speeches, dancing, and visiting.

# What Are Some Symbols of Independence Day?

The American flag and its red, white, and blue colors are symbols of Independence Day. Many people wear red, white, and blue clothing on Independence Day.

To some, the Declaration of Independence is a symbol of Independence Day. It helped form the United States. Another symbol of the holiday is the Liberty Bell. Colonists rang this large bell when the declaration was first read out loud in July 1776.

Patriotic songs are also important on Independence Day. Two favorites are "The Star-Spangled Banner" and "America the Beautiful."

◄ The Liberty Bell was put in place in 2003 at its new home in the Liberty Bell Center in Philadelphia, Pennsylvania.

# Do Other Countries Celebrate Their Independence?

Many other countries also have holidays to celebrate their independence.

In France, Bastille Day is July 14. It is similar to Independence Day. French people celebrate the beginning of their modern country. They go to parades, eat together, and watch fireworks.

On September 16, Mexicans celebrate the day they demanded freedom from Spain. They eat, listen to music, and dress in the colors of their flag.

Canadians celebrate their country's birthday on July 1. They watch fireworks, go to parades, and enjoy picnics on Canada Day.

◄ *With Canadian flags in her hair, a girl watches a Canada Day parade in Montreal.*

# What Does Independence Day Mean to Americans?

On Independence Day, Americans are thankful to be free. The United States is no longer ruled by another country. Americans can make their own choices about their lives.

Americans know that many people in history were not free. Some people around the world today are still not free.

People come together on Independence Day. They play outdoors and enjoy fireworks. Many people feel patriotic on Independence Day. They wave a flag and learn about their country's past. They are proud to be Americans.

◄ Children march in an Independence Day parade in Concord, California.

# Glossary

**anniversary**—a date people remember because an important event took place on that day

**bonfires**—large outdoor fires

**colonies**—territories settled by people from another country and ruled by that country

**colonists**—people who live in a newly settled area

**draft**—one version of a written work

**independence**—freedom

**patriotism**—loyal support for one's country

**traditions**—customs among a family or group

# Did You Know?

✴ The U.S. government made Independence Day an official holiday in 1941. However, Americans have celebrated Independence Day since 1777.

✴ Two of the men who wrote and signed the Declaration of Independence went on to be presidents of the United States. John Adams was the second president. Thomas Jefferson was the third.

✴ The British soldiers fighting in the Revolutionary War were called redcoats because of the color of their uniforms. The jackets they wore were red.

✴ Both John Adams and Thomas Jefferson died on July 4, 1826. That was the 50th anniversary of the adoption of the Declaration of Independence.

# Want to Know More?

## At the Library

Ansary, Mir Tamim. *Independence Day.* Chicago: Heinemann Library, 2002.

Frost, Helen. *Independence Day.* Mankato, Minn.: Pebble Books, 2000.

Schroeder, Holly. *The United States ABCs: A Book About the People and Places of the United States.* Minneapolis: Picture Window Books, 2004.

Ziefert, Harriet. *Hats Off for the Fourth of July.* New York: Viking, 2000.

## On the Web

For more information on *Independence Day,* use FactHound to track down Web sites related to this book.

1. Go to *www.facthound.com*
2. Type in a search word related to this book or this book ID: 0756507693.
3. Click on the *Fetch It* button.

Your trusty FactHound will fetch the best Web sites for you!

## On the Road

National Archives Building
700 Pennsylvania Ave. N.W.
Washington, DC 20408
866/272-6272
To see the Declaration of Independence and other historic documents

Liberty Bell Center
Independence National Historic Park
Sixth and Market Streets
Philadelphia, PA 19106
215/965-2305
To see the Liberty Bell and exhibits about its history

# Index

**About the Author**
Marc Tyler Nobleman has written more than 40 books for young readers. He has also written for a History Channel show called "The Great American History Quiz" and for several children's magazines including *Nickelodeon, Highlights for Children,* and *Read* (a Weekly Reader publication). He is also a cartoonist, and his single panels have appeared in more than 100 magazines internationally. He lives in Connecticut.